Questions & Answers
MAMMALS

Barbara Taylor

KINGFISHER

KINGFISHER
Kingfisher Publications Plc
New Penderel House
283–288 High Holborn
London WC1V 7HZ
www.kingfisherpub.com

Produced by Scintilla Editorial Ltd
33 Great Portland Street
London W1W 8QG
www.scintilla-editorial.co.uk

First published by Kingfisher Publications Plc in 2002
10 9 8 7 6 5 4 3 2 1

TS/0905/TIMS/UNI(MA)/130MA/F

Copyright © Kingfisher Publications Plc 2002

ISBN 0 7534 0707 8

Printed in China

Author: Barbara Taylor
Editors: John Birdsall, David Buxton and Hannah Wilson
Designers: Joe Conneally and Jane Tassie
Artwork archivists: Wendy Allison and Steve Robinson
Production: Debbie Otter

Contents

A World of Mammals

You are a mammal and so are dogs, cats, monkeys, elephants, kangaroos and whales. Mammals are named after female mammals' mammary glands, which produce milk to feed the young (right). Other mammal features are hair, a backbone, and lungs to breathe air.

How many mammals are there?

There are more than 4,000 different kinds, or 'species', of mammals. They are classified into 21 groups, called orders. Some orders contain just one species, others contain hundreds. The biggest is the 'rodents', which includes more than 1,700 species of mice, rats, chipmunks and squirrels, and the 'bats', which has nearly 1,000 species.

Striped field mouse

Are mammals clever?

Mammals are the most intelligent animals alive. The cleverest mammals are primates, such as humans and apes. These mammals can learn new things and pass on information to others. They spend many years caring for and teaching their young. Some primates, such as humans and chimpanzees (below), make and use tools.

Are all mammals similar in size?

Mammals span an enormous range of sizes, shapes and weights. The largest creature ever to inhabit Earth is the blue whale (above), which can grow up to 33 metres long and may weigh almost 150 tonnes — the equivalent of about 30 African elephants. The world's smallest mammal, and one of the rarest, is the tiny Kitti's hog-nosed bat. This bat has a body the size of a bumblebee and weighs in at two grammes or less.

Camel
Moose
Bison
Polar bear
Tiger

What makes mammals special?

Mammals are the only animals that have hair. The hair grows out of little pits in the skin to make fur coats, wool, whiskers, prickles and spines. Bears (right), tigers and gorillas have very thick fur coats. Other mammals such as whales, elephants, hippos and people have very little hair. Hair helps keep mammals warm and dry.

Brown bear

Which mammals can fly?

The only mammals capable of true flight are bats. They have wings made of skin stretched between their finger bones. In order to fly, a bat flexes its arms and moves them up and down. A few mammals, such as flying squirrels, have skin stretched between their front and back legs, but they can only glide through the air for short distances.

Fruit bat

Giraffe

Walrus   Gorilla   Hippopotamus   Rhinoceros

African elephant

Early Mammals

The first mammals were small, shrew-like creatures that evolved from reptiles some 200 million years ago. When the dinosaurs became extinct, mammals quickly evolved into shapes and sizes that equipped them for life in almost every habitat. Mammals have been the dominant form of life on Earth ever since.

Which animals did mammals evolve from?

Mammals evolved from what are known as 'mammal-like reptiles'. The earliest of these were the pelycosaurs, or 'sail reptiles', such as the predatory *Dimetrodon* (right). Scientists believe that *Dimetrodon's* sail was used like a solar panel, so the large reptile would warm up quickly. After the pelycosaurs came the therapsids and then the dog-like cynodonts. Cynodonts are the direct ancestors of mammals and may have been warm-blooded.

Did the first horses have hoofs?

The first horse, called *Hyracotherium*, was about the size of a dog. Instead of hoofs, it had four toes on its front feet and three toes on its back feet. Modern horses are much larger and have only one toe on each foot so they can run faster.

Did mammals live with dinosaurs?

Dinosaurs appeared at the start of the Triassic period, only 20 million years before the first mammals evolved. For the next 135 million years, mammals and dinosaurs lived side by side – although the dinosaurs would hardly have noticed the small, largely nocturnal creatures that scurried about their feet.

What did the first mammals look like?

The first mammals, such as *Megazostrodon*, were tiny, secretive animals that scurried around under the feet of the dinosaurs or climbed through the trees. They were only about five centimetres long, and looked rather like the tree shrews alive today. Early mammals probably came out at night to avoid predators and to hunt for insects using their keen sense of smell.

Which early cats had teeth like daggers?

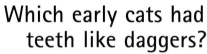

More heavily built than a modern lion, and with huge, dagger-like canine teeth, sabre-toothed cats, such as *Smilodon* (right), were formidable predators that could attack prey as large as bison and giant ground sloths. They didn't use their oversized teeth for biting, but for stabbing the soft belly or throat of their victims. Sabre-toothed cats had enormous front neck muscles enabling them to stab down hard and keep their jaws open wide.

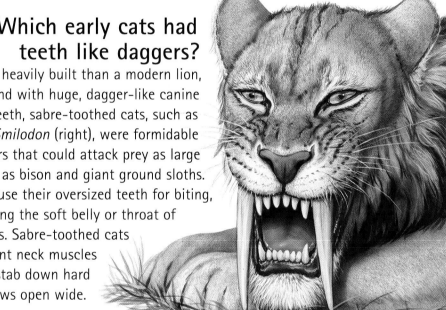

Why did mammoths have long hair?

Unlike the African and Indian elephants of today, mammoths lived in cold areas and needed their long, shaggy coats to keep warm. Standing more than three metres tall, their huge bulk also helped them to conserve heat. African elephants today have large ears to lose heat, whereas mammoths had smaller ears to reduce heat loss.

7

Fur Coats

Most mammals are covered in fur or hair made of a tough protein called keratin. The hair in the coat traps a layer of air and helps to protect the mammal from cold, heat, wind and water. Stiff hairs called whiskers serve as touch organs, while spiny hairs are useful for defence.

How do mammals clean their fur?

To keep their fur clean and free from parasites such as fleas, mammals lick their fur with their tongues, comb through it with their fingers and nibble it with their teeth. This is called grooming. It also helps a mammal such as the otter to keep its coat both waterproof and warm. Social animals, such as chimpanzees (left), often groom each other's fur. As well as helping to clean parts of the coat that are difficult to reach, social grooming can strengthen friendships, keeping the group together.

Which mammals have hardly any hair?

Rhinos, elephants and hippos have only a sparse covering of hair because they live in such hot climates. Sea mammals such as dolphins (below) and whales also have very little hair, but this is because they need to be streamlined in the water. Instead of fur, they have a thick layer of fat to keep them warm. The very strange naked mole rat is also almost entirely hairless, because it lives in underground burrows that stay warm all the time.

Where did mammal hair come from?

As the early mammals evolved from reptiles, the characteristic reptilian scales slowly changed into individual fibres that eventually became hair. The pangolin, however, in its coat of overlapping scales still looks remarkably reptilian, but the scales are, in fact, made up of densely massed hair. Similarly, a rhino's horn is not horn at all – it's hair.

Cape pangolin

Which mammal has the longest hair?

Many animals that live in cold northern or Alpine climates have long coats, but the musk ox has the longest coat of all. Some of the hairs in its outer coat can reach almost one metre long. The musk ox also has a dense undercoat of short, soft hair that is eight times warmer than sheep's wool. Together the insulating layers protect the musk ox from the freezing arctic winter. As summer approaches, however, it sheds its dense winter coat to prevent overheating.

Which mammals have spiny hairs?

Echidnas (below), porcupines, hedgehogs and some tenrecs (hedgehog-like mammals from Madagascar) have stiff, sharp spines on their backs to deter predators. If an echidna is threatened, it digs down into the dirt to hide its soft underside, with only its spines visible. A hedgehog can roll itself into a prickly ball to protect its soft underparts. The young of these spiny mammals are born with soft spines that harden as they grow older.

Why do some mammals turn white in winter?

Mammals that live in cold places, such as arctic foxes or stoats (left), may change the colour of their coats so that they are well camouflaged all year. In winter, they grow thick white coats that make them hard to see against a snowy background. In summer, their white fur is replaced by a thinner coat of brown or grey.

Eyes, Ears and Noses

A mammal's senses of sight, hearing, smell, touch and taste help it to locate food, avoid danger, find its way around and to look for a mate. Most mammals see the world only in black and white, but have highly sensitive noses. Many nocturnal mammals also have a super-sharp sense of hearing.

Is a trunk a nose?
An elephant's trunk is actually an elongation of both its upper lip and nose. The result is a versatile 'limb' that is highly sensitive to smell and touch and that can suck up water to drink and tear edible leaves from the branches of tall trees.

Daytime – narrow pupils   Night-time – wide pupils

Why do a cat's eyes shine in the dark?
A cat is a night hunter and, in low light, its pupils open very wide (above right) to let as much light as possible reach the eyes' receptors. Any light rays that miss the receptors are reflected back by a mirror-like layer called the 'tapetum lucidum' at the back of the eye. This gives the receptors a second chance to absorb the rays. It is this layer that makes a cat's eyes shine when it is caught in a bright light at night.

Why is a pig's nose flat?
Pigs have an excellent sense of smell, and their flat noses are very sensitive at the tip. The shape of their noses helps them to turn over the soil and sniff out roots, insect larvae and other food. In France, pigs are used to find truffles, a type of fungi that grows under the ground. Female pigs are chosen for this job because the fungi smell like male pigs and so the females are attracted to them!

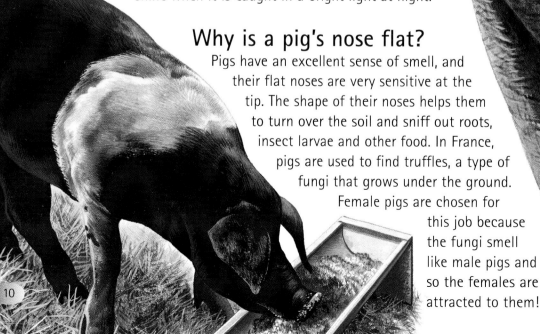

How does a dolphin 'see' with sound?

When dolphins are hunting fish, they make high-pitched clicking sounds. The Amazon River dolphin sends out up to 80 clicks per second. These clicking sounds are reflected by objects in the dolphin's path and bounce back as echoes. The echoes help the dolphin to work out where the fish are and how far away they are. This technique is called 'echo-location' and is also used by whales and bats.

Sound waves reflected back from prey

Quick-fire Quiz

1. **Where does the jackrabbit live?**
   a) In the arctic tundra
   b) In the rainforest
   c) In the desert

2. **What is the tapetum lucidum?**
   a) A layer at the back of the eyes
   b) A bone in the inner ear
   c) A sense organ in the snout of a mole

3. **What is the scientific name for 'whiskers'?**
   a) Fibroids
   b) Vibrissae
   c) Antennae

4. **What is a dolphin's sound sense called?**
   a) Click-location
   b) Pitch-location
   c) Echo-location

How does a mole find its food?

Living almost all of its life underground, the mole has to rely on its senses of touch and smell. Sensitive hairs and special touch organs in its snout, together with its keen sense of smell, help it find the beetles and earthworms that it eats.

Why do many mammals have long whiskers?

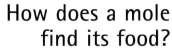

Most mammals, such as cats and rats (left), have long, stiff, hairs that protrude from the fur on their face, muzzle and lower legs. These 'vibrissae', or 'whiskers', are attached to nerves in the skin and allow the animal to 'feel' nearby objects before touching them. Nocturnal mammals use their whiskers to judge the width of narrow spaces and to help them find their way about in the dark. The vibrissae of water mammals can also detect subtle changes in water currents as well as the movement of prey in dark or muddy waters.

Why does a jackrabbit have huge ears?

The jackrabbit's long ears not only allow it to listen out for enemies, but also help it to control its body temperature. The jackrabbit lives in the desert, where it is very hot by day and very cold at night. By controlling the flow of blood through the many blood vessels in its large, thin ears, the jackrabbit can lose heat when it is hot, or take in heat when it is cold, and so maintain a balanced temperature.

Run, Jump, Climb and Fly

Humans are the only mammals that walk on two legs all the time. Most mammals walk on four legs. Some, like bears, put their feet flat on the ground, while cats and dogs move on their toes, and horses and deer walk on their toenails. The only mammals that can fly are bats, but most can swim – whales and seals swim even better than fish!

Are sloths really slothful?

Sloths don't do anything quickly. They spend about 20 hours a day snoozing in the trees of the rainforest. Sloths have long, strong claws that hook around the branches so tightly that they do not fall off even if they go to sleep. When they do creep about to feed or expel waste, sloths only reach speeds of about two metres per minute. One of the benefits of their sluggish lifestyle, however, is that it helps to keep them hidden from airborne predators such as eagles.

Which mammals are champion jumpers?

Kangaroos (left) can jump farther than any other animal. Their legs are so powerful that they can cover 14 metres in a single hop and leap up vertically more than three metres in the air. Kangaroos also use their enormous feet like springboards to bound along at speeds of up to 48 km/h. When travelling at high speed, a kangaroo's long, heavy tail is held out behind it to help balance the weight of its body.

Which is the fastest mammal?

1 The cheetah is the fastest land animal over short distances. It can sprint at speeds of more than 100 km/h, but has to stop after about a minute – it gets too hot!

2 A cheetah's speed comes from its long, powerful legs and the large muscles along its back, which it flexes like a spring with each long, explosive stride.

3 The cheetah is the only cat unable to retract its claws. It uses them to grip the ground when running – like a pair of spiked running shoes. The claws are fairly blunt, but very strong.

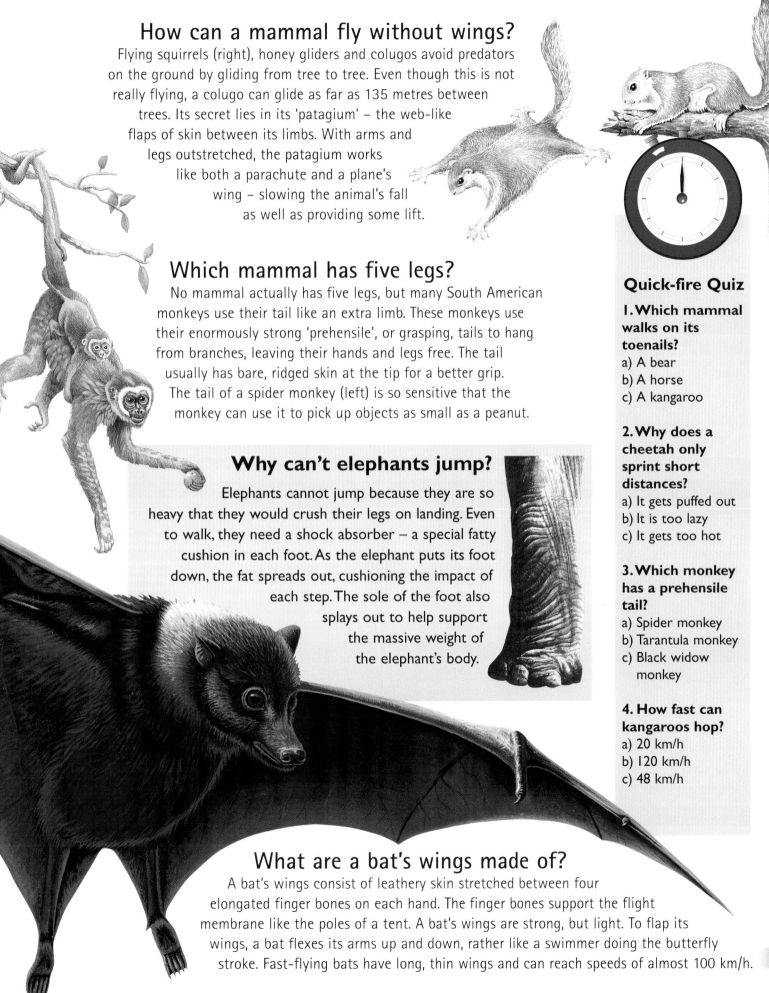

How can a mammal fly without wings?

Flying squirrels (right), honey gliders and colugos avoid predators on the ground by gliding from tree to tree. Even though this is not really flying, a colugo can glide as far as 135 metres between trees. Its secret lies in its 'patagium' – the web-like flaps of skin between its limbs. With arms and legs outstretched, the patagium works like both a parachute and a plane's wing – slowing the animal's fall as well as providing some lift.

Which mammal has five legs?

No mammal actually has five legs, but many South American monkeys use their tail like an extra limb. These monkeys use their enormously strong 'prehensile', or grasping, tails to hang from branches, leaving their hands and legs free. The tail usually has bare, ridged skin at the tip for a better grip. The tail of a spider monkey (left) is so sensitive that the monkey can use it to pick up objects as small as a peanut.

Why can't elephants jump?

Elephants cannot jump because they are so heavy that they would crush their legs on landing. Even to walk, they need a shock absorber – a special fatty cushion in each foot. As the elephant puts its foot down, the fat spreads out, cushioning the impact of each step. The sole of the foot also splays out to help support the massive weight of the elephant's body.

Quick-fire Quiz

1. Which mammal walks on its toenails?
a) A bear
b) A horse
c) A kangaroo

2. Why does a cheetah only sprint short distances?
a) It gets puffed out
b) It is too lazy
c) It gets too hot

3. Which monkey has a prehensile tail?
a) Spider monkey
b) Tarantula monkey
c) Black widow monkey

4. How fast can kangaroos hop?
a) 20 km/h
b) 120 km/h
c) 48 km/h

What are a bat's wings made of?

A bat's wings consist of leathery skin stretched between four elongated finger bones on each hand. The finger bones support the flight membrane like the poles of a tent. A bat's wings are strong, but light. To flap its wings, a bat flexes its arms up and down, rather like a swimmer doing the butterfly stroke. Fast-flying bats have long, thin wings and can reach speeds of almost 100 km/h.

Food and Feeding

Mammals must eat regularly to maintain a warm body temperature, and small mammals need to eat more often than large ones. Most mammals have three kinds of teeth — incisors, canines and molars.

Are koalas fussy eaters?

Koalas (right) eat only the leaves of a few kinds of eucalyptus, or 'gum' tree. They also need to choose fresh young leaves because the older leaves contain poisons. Koalas spend three-quarters of their lives asleep because their food provides very little energy.

How does a tiger kill its prey?

A tiger's main hunting skills are silence and stealth. Its stripes camouflage the tiger so that it can creep up on its prey without being seen. The tiger's jaws contain long, pointed front teeth, which it uses to stab prey, and its sharp hooked claws and powerful shoulders help it to cling on tightly and pull the prey to the ground.

1 After spotting its prey, the tiger crouches close to the ground. Then it creeps forwards slowly.

2 When it is just a few metres away, the tiger makes a sudden, powerful rush and then pounces.

Why does a giraffe have such a long neck?

A giraffe's long neck and legs help it to eat fresh new leaves high in the trees that other animals cannot reach. A giraffe is about six metres tall, but it can reach even higher by sticking out its 50-centimetre-long, blue tongue and using it to pull off leaves.

How does a honey badger find honey?

The ratel, or honey badger, (above) and a bird called the honey guide are both very fond of honey. The bird shows the honey badger the way to a bee's nest and waits for the badger to dig out the nest with its strong claws. Then they both share the feast.

Why does a vampire bat drink blood?

Blood is a rich source of food that is not used by many animals. However, the common vampire bat lives on nothing else. The bat feeds mainly on the blood of cattle (left) – not human blood! To feed, it creeps up to its victim and cuts open a flap of skin with its razor-sharp teeth. It then laps up the blood with its tongue. Chemicals in the saliva stop the blood clotting. The bat drinks about two tablespoons of blood each night.

Quick-fire Quiz

1. Which leaves do koalas eat?
a) Willow
b) Eucalyptus
c) Oak

2. How much blood does a vampire bat drink each night?
a) Five teaspoonfuls
b) One cupful
c) Two tablespoons

3. Why is a tiger striped?
a) For decoration
b) To attract a mate
c) For camouflage

4. Which of these mammals is a carnivore?
a) Tiger
b) Giraffe
c) Koala

3 Using its powerful paws, the tiger grips its prey and kills it with a bite to the neck.

Do teeth and jaws reveal what a mammal eats?

Most mammals are herbivores, or plant-eaters. They have long jaws with forward-pointing incisors that slice through their food, and long rows of flat-topped molar teeth to grind it to a pulp. Carnivores, or meat-eaters, have short, powerful jaws with long, stabbing canine teeth and shearing cheek teeth to slice meat or crack bones. Omnivores, which eat meat and plants, have a mixture of teeth to cope with their varied diet.

Herbivore   Carnivore

Carnivore   Omnivore (human)

Combat and Attack

The main reason mammals attack other animals is to catch and kill them for food. But occasionally, mammals attack others of their own kind, either to claim their own patch of ground or to win a mate. These fights can be fierce – claws and teeth can inflict severe damage and even cause death. More often, however, they are simply shows of aggression or trials of strength that avoid serious injury.

Why do hippos have big teeth?

Male hippos fight to defend either a territory or the right to mate with the females within that territory. First, they threaten each other by grunting, scattering dung with their tails and by showing off their huge canine teeth, or 'tusks'. But if neither hippo gives up, the rivals fight, lunging at each other with their razor-sharp tusks, which can grow up to 50 centimetres long. Nasty wounds are often inflicted, and hippos may even kill each other in these ferocious battles.

Why do young mammals play-fight?

Many young mammals such as lion cubs, fox cubs and baby gorillas (right) often have pretend fights with their brothers and sisters. They practise how to pin each other down and use their teeth and claws. The youngsters do not usually hurt each other in these fights, but this kind of combat provides valuable training for the day when they have to fend for themselves. Some of the skills they learn will help them hunt, whereas others equip them for battles with rivals of their own kind.

Why do horses fight?

Horses, in common with most grazing animals, are not particularly aggressive mammals. If a predator, such as a big cat, threatens a herd of horses, they will gallop away on their long legs rather than stand and fight. But fights can and do break out between rival males, or stallions, when they are competing for a mate. Most battles begin with a little bit of pushing and shoving, and if one of the males is clearly stronger, the competition usually ends there. But if the contestants are evenly matched, then the fight can become ugly as the competing males rear, bite and kick out at each other, often inflicting nasty wounds.

Why do female reindeer have antlers?

Female reindeer, or caribou, are the only female deer to have antlers. The most likely reason for this is that the females need the antlers to fight for food. In winter, when the deer have to dig away the snow to find the vegetation below, having antlers helps them to compete with the males. In other deer, such as red deer (right), it is only the males that have antlers and they are used as weapons to fight rivals in the breeding season, or 'rut'. Competing males lock their antlers together and push against each other until the weaker deer gives up and runs away. The victor wins the right to mate with the female deer.

How do antlers grow?

The antlers of male deer are often damaged during fights, so they grow a new set each year. The antlers fall off after the rut and a few weeks later, the new set start to show as small knobs on the top of the head. The growing antlers are covered in a soft skin called velvet. Underneath the velvet, tiny blood vessels feed the growing antlers until just before the next rut when the blood supply is cut off. The velvet dries up and peels off and the deer rub it off on bushes and trees. Young deer may take five years to develop a full set of antlers, each year producing an increasingly larger set (right).

1 year

3 years

5 years

Quick-fire Quiz

1. How often do deer shed their antlers?
a) Every ten years
b) Once in a lifetime
c) Every year

2. Which kind of teeth are a hippo's tusks?
a) Canine teeth
b) Incisor teeth
c) Molar teeth

3. Why does an elephant seal have a 'trunk'?
a) To squirt water
b) To make loud noises
c) To pick up food

4. What is an adult male horse called?
a) A colt
b) A stallion
c) A mustang

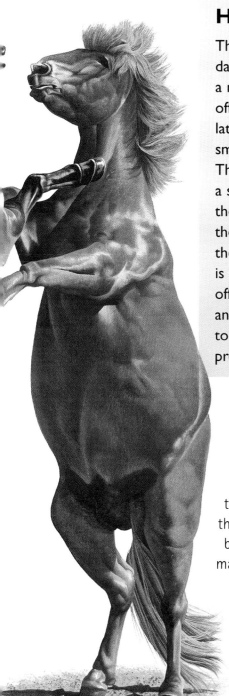

Why are male elephant seals so big?

Male elephant seals are at least three times the weight of the females and are the largest of all seals. Males are so big because they fight to win the right to mate with up to 100 females. Using an inflatable 'trunk' as a loudspeaker, the males roar challenges at their rivals. Much of the fighting is only a show of strength, but the seals' sharp teeth can cause serious injuries, and some weaker males may even be killed.

Defence

To avoid its enemies, a mammal may keep very still and hide, or run away as fast as it can. A social mammal may seek safety in numbers to protect itself and its young. Clever tricks such as pretending to be dead or rolling up into an armoured ball may also help a solitary creature to survive an attack. A few mammals, however, protect themselves rather more aggressively with sharp spines and chemical sprays!

Why is a porcupine spiny?

Porcupines, such as the crested porcupine (right), have coats containing hard, sharp-tipped hairs called quills. These can be up to 35 centimetres long, and provide a useful deterrent to predators. If threatened, a porcupine will turn its back, rattle its quills, grunt and stamp its feet. If the enemy is not discouraged, the porcupine runs backwards at them. Its spines are quite loosely attached, so some will stick in the attacker's skin and may cause nasty wounds.

How do musk oxen protect their young?

If a group of musk oxen are attacked, they gather in a tight circle with their massive pointed horns facing outwards. The females and young are protected in the middle of the circle. Providing none of the oxen panic and break ranks, this defensive tactic is extremely effective, especially for large winter herds, but it can work even for small summer herds of only ten or so.

Why do fawns have spotted coats?

Young mammals are often at the greatest risk from predators. Not as strong or quick on their feet as their parents, the best defence for many youngsters is to hide. They often rely on their cleverly coloured coats to camouflage them from view. For this reason, the fawns of many deer, such as the roe (left), have spotted coats for the first year or so of their lives.

Which mammals wear a suit of armour?

The top side of an armadillo's body is covered with bony plates joined together with flexible skin. A large shield protects the armadillo's head. To protect their soft undersides, some armadillos, such as the nine-banded armadillo (above left), pull in their legs so their armour clamps firmly against the ground. Others, such as the three-banded armadillos (above right), roll themselves up into a tight ball. They can leave a small opening in their plates to snap shut on a predator's paw or snout.

Why do opossums pretend to be dead?

Most predators prefer to eat prey they have killed themselves and will ignore a 'meal' that is already dead. The Virginia opossum of North America takes advantage of this fact by playing dead when danger threatens. If it sees a predator, it lies on its back and keeps very still, even defecating to produce an off-putting odour. This play-acting can last for hours, but when the danger is over, the opossum miraculously comes back to life!

Why is the skunk so smelly?

The skunk's striking black and white colours are intended to warn enemies to stay away. But if a skunk is threatened, it stamps its feet, fluffs up its tail and fur, and may even do a handstand to make itself look bigger and more frightening! If the intruder is not deterred, the skunk will drop back onto all fours and squirt a horrible, smelly liquid from two glands – like tiny water pistols – in its rear end . The liquid burns the skin and stings the eyes. While the attacker coughs and chokes, the skunk makes its getaway. People who are sprayed by skunks often have to throw away their clothes because the smell is so bad!

Birth and Babies

Mammal babies may develop in three quite different ways. A few mammals, such as the platypus (below), hatch out of soft-shelled eggs. In pouched mammals, such as the kangaroo, the young are born in a very undeveloped state and then continue to develop in their mother's pouch. In most mammals, including humans, the young stay inside their mother's body, taking in nourishment until they are more fully developed and ready to be born.

Which mammals lay eggs?

Only three mammals lay eggs – the platypus (left) and two kinds of echidna, or spiny anteater. Called 'monotremes', these mammals all live in Australia and New Guinea. The eggs have soft shells, like those of a reptile. Platypuses incubate their eggs in a nest, curling up around them for about three weeks. Echidnas keep their eggs warm in a pouch. When the eggs hatch, the baby mammals suck milk that oozes through the skin on their mother's belly – she does not have teats.

Which mammals are born underwater?

Whales, dolphins (below), dugongs and manatees all give birth underwater. A birth usually takes place in warm water close to the surface, so the baby can surface quickly and start breathing. The new baby may be helped to the surface by its mother or other members of its group. Suckling takes place underwater too. Milk is squirted into the baby's mouth from the mother's teats. It has a high fat and protein content, which helps the youngster to grow quickly.

Which mammals are helpless when they are born?

Many mammals including mice, dormice, hamsters, rats and rabbits are born without any hair or fur. Unable to see or hear, they are totally dependent on their mother. They rely on the warmth of her body and a cosy nest to keep warm.

Which babies can run as soon as they are born?

Hoofed mammals that live in open country, such as zebras, wildebeest and caribou, give birth to remarkably well-developed young that are up and about almost at once. This is because these animals are always at risk from predators, and the young are especially vulnerable. There is safety in numbers so their only defence is to run with the herd. A zebra foal can run away from danger only an hour or so after being born. Wildebeest calves can stand just three to five minutes after being born, and are up and running with the herd half an hour later!

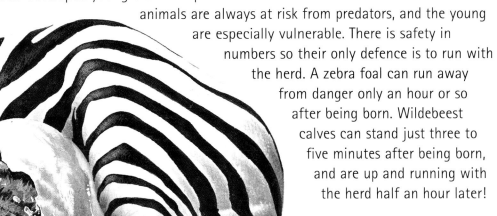

How long do baby mammals take to grow up?

Mammals such as cats and gerbils care for their young for just a few weeks, whereas apes, humans and elephants look after their offspring for many years. Almost all young mammals are reared by their mothers – not their fathers – because they are dependent on their mother's milk. Apes, such as chimpanzees, gorillas and orang-utans (above), do not become independent of their mothers until they are about eight years old. Before this age, they have to learn how to climb, find food and defend themselves, as well as how to behave with others of their own kind. Part of this learning happens during play.

Which babies live in pouches?

Most 'marsupials', or pouched mammals, such as kangaroos, wombats and opossums, live in Australia and New Guinea. At birth, the babies are blind, naked and extremely tiny – a baby kangaroo would fit on a teaspoon! Yet these delicate babies have to squirm and wriggle over their mother's body to find her pouch. The only help she gives them is to lick a path through her fur for the baby to follow. The young have large, strong front legs to help them make this dangerous journey. Once inside the pouch, the young clamps onto a teat to drink its mother's milk. It stays warm and safe like this for weeks or months while it does most of its growing up. A baby grey kangaroo stays in its mother's pouch for 300 days.

Living in Groups

Group living has many advantages for mammals. Members of a group can help each other to find food, fight predators and to protect and care for the young. Within a group, some animals are more important than others. Leaders can be male (as in a group of gorillas), female (elephants) or an equal pair (wolves).

Which wolf is top dog?

A top male and a top female wolf lead a wolf pack together. The other wolves all have their own ranks below the top pair. High-ranking wolves stand tall with their ears and tail up. They may show their teeth and growl (above right). Low-ranking wolves whine and crouch down with their tail between their legs when they meet a higher-ranking member of their group (above left).

How do killer whales help each other?

A group of killer whales stays together for life and the bonds between the animals in a group are very strong. They help each other to hunt and trap seals, squid, fish and other whales, coordinating their movements and activities with a special whale language of underwater whistles, clicks and honks.

Why do lions live in prides?

Lions are unusual among cats because they live in family groups, called prides. This allows them to hunt together and catch bigger prey. They also look after each other's cubs, which means more young survive. A typical pride contains 12 related females and their cubs. A single male usually leads the group and protects it from other males. In return, the male often eats first, even though females do most of the hunting.

Why do groups of mammals migrate?

Seasonal change in the food supply is one of the main reasons for mammal migration. In the dry season, when grass supplies have been used up, more than one million wildebeest (below) trek across the African plains to find fresh new grass that has sprouted in areas of greater rainfall. Caribou, or reindeer, travel longer distances than wildebeest — up to 9,000 kilometres a year across the frozen wastes of the north. Grey whales travel farther still — each year, they journey from the equator to the Arctic and back.

Which names describe some groups of mammals?

A troop of gorillas, a herd of elephants, a pack of wolves and a pride of lions are some of the more familiar names for mammals living in groups. But have you heard of a colony of bats, a town of prairie dogs, a crash of rhinos, a school of dolphins, a clan of hyenas, a mob of kangaroos, a kindle of kittens or a leap of leopards? When a group of camels travels with people, the whole group is called a caravan of camels.

Quick-fire Quiz

1. What is a group of dolphins called?
a) A class
b) A school
c) A university

2. Which lions usually eat first?
a) Males
b) Females
c) Cubs

3. How long does a group of killer whales stay together?
a) One year
b) Ten years
c) For life

4. How far do caribou migrate?
a) 90,000 km
b) 9,000 km
c) 1,000 km

Why do meerkats need lookouts?

Meerkats are a type of mongoose that live in groups of 50 or more in a network of burrows. Group members take it in turns to do different jobs, such as finding food or acting as lookouts. Often, most of the group is busy finding food, so lookouts are needed to scan the surroundings for predators such as eagles and snakes. If a lookout senses danger, it barks out a warning and the whole group quickly bolts to the safety of the nearest hole.

Keeping in Touch

Howling wolves, roaring lions, trumpeting elephants – we are not the only mammals to 'talk' to each other. As well as using sounds to communicate, mammals also leave messages by making scent marks that others of their own kind can sniff and understand. Body language, such as pulling faces or raising tails, is another form of mammal communication.

Why do humpback whales sing to each other?

In the breeding season, male humpback whales sing long and complicated songs. This may be to attract a mate or to warn other males to keep out of their area. Humpback whales often keep singing for a day or more, repeating the same song. The sound of their underwater love songs can carry through the water for 30 kilometres or more.

Which is the noisiest mammal?

Howler monkeys (below) are named after their roaring calls, which are among the loudest and most frequent of any animal. Males and females howl, but males make louder calls because they have a large chamber in the throat that increases the volume of the call. Howling helps each troop of howlers to work out where other troops are so they can space themselves out through the forest and avoid unecessary fights.

Why don't seal pups get lost in a crowd?

At a breeding colony, female seals all give birth to their pups at the same time. At some colonies thousands of pups are crowded closely together on the seashore. After feeding her pup for a time, each mother needs to leave her youngster and go to sea to find food for herself. When she returns, she has to locate her own pup among all the others on the shore. She does this by using her sharp hearing to listen for the special, unique cry that each pup makes while waiting for its mother to reappear. When the pup is found, she sniffs it, confirming its identity by its individual scent.

How do primates warn each other of danger?

Primates, such as monkeys, chimps (right) and other apes, are among the best of all mammal communicators. Many live in scattered groups in the trees, so when danger threatens, all the members need to know about it as quickly as possible. When alarmed, they warn each other by attracting attention in different ways. They may jump up and down on the spot, rush through the trees, shaking leaves and breaking branches, or scream and bark loudly. Their calls can even reveal whether the danger comes from the ground or the air.

Why do mammals leave scent marks?

Some mammals, such as cats and dogs, make chemicals called pheromones in special scent glands. The glands are found on various parts of the body such as the feet. The scent is 'posted' on trees or the ground as the animal moves around, leaving smelly messages for others to 'read'. Scent gives information about age, gender, health and social status. A scent message may say 'keep out of my territory', or 'I am looking for a mate'.

Quick-fire Quiz

1. Which monkeys make loud calls?
a) Shouters
b) Roarers
c) Howlers

2. How far can the song of a humpback whale travel in water?
a) 300 km
b) 30 km
c) 3 km

3. How do female seals find their own pups in a crowd?
a) By sight
b) By sound and smell
c) By touch

4. What does a frightened chimp do?
a) Grin
b) Relax
c) Close lips tightly

Why do wolves howl?

The howling of a wolf pack carries for several kilometres and warns other wolves to keep out of a pack's territory. Howling helps a separated wolf to relocate its pack. Wolves also howl before hunting – this may help to strengthen their bonds before the hunt.

Why do chimps pull faces?

Chimps pull faces and make a variety of sounds to show other chimps in a group how they feel. When a chimp is frightened or excited, it lets others know by making a 'fear grin', which looks like a smile to us. A wide open and relaxed mouth is a play face, which might be used during a game. An angry chimp clenches its lips tightly shut.

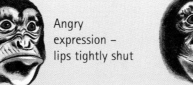

Play face – mouth open, top teeth mostly covered

Fear grin – mouth wide open, all teeth bared

Angry expression – lips tightly shut

Relaxed or concentrating – mouth closed

Mammal Homes

Mammals build homes to protect themselves and their young from predators and the weather. Some of them, such as rabbits, badgers and foxes, dig underground burrows. Other mammals build their homes above ground, using leaves, sticks or grass. But the champion mammal home-maker is the beaver, which builds an incredibly elaborate home called a lodge.

Do bears always sleep in caves?

During the winter, when food becomes scarce, bears in northern lands seek out a cave or large burrow where they can doze through the coldest months (right). Female polar bears dig cosy snow dens in which to spend their winter. There they can also give birth safely to their cubs in the spring. It is important that the den is snug as bears need to stay warm while they sleep.

Which mammals live in towns?

North American prairie dogs live in large underground burrows called 'towns' (below). The largest reported town was estimated to contain about 400 million prairie dogs and to extend over an area of 65,000 square kilometres. However, numbers in a town today are usually no more than one thousand. Prairie dogs, which are actually a kind of ground squirrel, live in family units, called coteries, made up of an adult male, several adult females and their young. Because prairie dog towns are so large, it would be easy to imagine that these squirrels are extremely sociable. In fact, each coterie defends its burrows very aggressively and neighbours frequently squabble.

Why does a dormouse sleep through the winter?

In winter, when the weather is cold and food becomes impossible to find, the dormouse goes into a deep sleep called hibernation. During this time, the temperature of the dormouse drops to almost that of the air around it, and its bodily functions almost stop. This slow-down allows the dormouse to survive all winter on the fat stored in its body.

Which mammals live in wheat fields?

The tiny harvest mouse lives among tall grasses and crops. Here, it builds both 'day' nests and more complex 'nurseries', by weaving together the leaves of living plants. The globe-shaped nests are lined with shredded leaves to make them warm.

Why is a beaver's home like a castle?

A beaver's home, or lodge, (below) is a clever construction of logs, mud and stones. It even has an underwater entrance. Using the same building materials, the beaver also builds dams to create a pond around its lodge. Like the moat around a castle, the pond makes it difficult for predators such as wolves and bears to attack the beaver's home.

Quick-fire Quiz

1. What is a beaver's home called?
a) A castle
b) A fortress
c) A lodge

2. How many prairie dogs lived in the largest-ever town?
a) 400 million
b) 1 million
c) 100 million

3. What is a deep sleep in winter called?
a) Migration
b) Hibernation
c) Slumberation

4. What does a harvest mouse line its nest with?
a) Feathers
b) Soft fur
c) Shredded leaves

Rabbit warren

Mole hill

Why do mammals live underground?

Most small mammals make underground homes to be safe from larger predators – a rabbit digs a network of tunnels called a warren (left). At dusk, rabbits come out to feed and drink. The mole, however, spends almost all of its life under the ground, 'swimming' through the soil with its shovel-like feet. It eats worms that fall into its tunnels and stores surplus worms in a 'larder'. In soft soil, the mole pushes the soil up into a ridge above its body. In hard soil, it pushes up excess soil to make a familiar 'mole hill' (left).

Birth chamber

Coping with Extremes

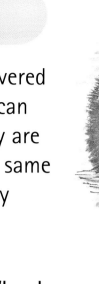

Mammals live all over the world, from ice-covered mountain tops to baking hot deserts. They can survive in extreme conditions partly because they are warm-blooded. Their body temperature stays the same even when their surroundings are very hot or very cold. But to help them cope with extreme climates, mammals often have special adaptations, such as extra-large hearts, thick fur or huge ears that give off heat.

How do llamas live high on mountains?

The llama is a member of the camel family along with vicunas and alpacas. It lives in the Andes of South America at heights of up to 5,000 metres (left). The llama's thick fur keeps it warm and its blood is good at taking in oxygen from the thin mountain air. Leathery pads on the sole of its feet give the llama excellent grip on the steep slopes.

Why are whales so fat?

The thick layer of fat, or 'blubber', under a whale's skin helps to keep out the cold of polar oceans, where water temperatures are often below freezing. The blubber can be up to 50 centimetres thick in some whales. Blubber is so good at keeping body heat in that whales could overheat in warm weather or after lots of activity. To avoid this happening, blood can be pumped through blood vessels running through the blubber near the skin surface, where it is cooled by the water.

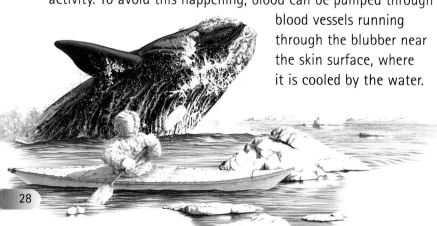

Why do macaques take hot baths?

Some Japanese macaques (above) live in the far north of Japan where winters are very cold and snowy. To escape the biting cold, they sit up to their necks in hot volcanic springs. These hot baths, together with their very thick fur coats, keep them warm even when they are surrounded by snow and ice. No other monkey is able to live this far north and endure such extremes of temperature.

How do camels cope with life in the desert?

Camels (below) are adapted to desert life from head to toe. Their nostrils can be closed – not only to keep out sand, but also to help prevent water loss in their breath. Camels can further reduce water loss by producing little urine and by allowing their body temperature to rise, which means that they will sweat only when they get extremely hot. The humps contain stores of energy-rich fat that allow the camel to survive for weeks without food. Camels also have unusually splayed feet, and walk on their sole-pads not their hoofs. This stops them sinking in soft sand.

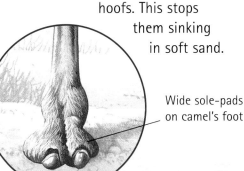

Wide sole-pads on camel's foot

Why do fennec foxes and kit foxes look so alike?

The fennec fox and the kit fox look very similar, yet they are not related and live in different parts of the world. The fennec fox lives in Africa and the kit fox lives in North America. They look alike because they have both adapted to the same sort of harsh desert conditions. Both foxes are quite small (the fennec fox is the smallest of all foxes), as food is scarce in their dry habitats, and both have big ears which they use to locate prey and keep cool. The similarity is known as convergent evolution.

Fennec fox   Kit fox

How does a kangaroo rat manage to survive without drinking?

The kangaroo rat of North America gets most of the water it needs from the seeds, grasses and herbs that it eats. To conserve moisture, it stays in its burrow during the hot desert days only coming out at night, when it is cooler. The kangaroo rat also has special kidneys that need less water to process waste – so it produces very dry droppings!

Quick-fire Quiz

1. Which part of its feet does a camel walk on?
a) Its hoofs
b) Its sole-pads
c) Its heels

2. How thick can whale blubber be?
a) 5 cm
b) 50 m
c) 50 cm

3. Where do llamas live?
a) The Andes
b) The Alps
c) The Himalayas

4. When are kangaroo rats active?
a) At night
b) By day
c) In winter

Water Mammals

Mammals live in the salty water of seas and oceans as well as freshwater rivers and lakes. Some, such as dolphins, spend all their lives in the water. Others, including otters, visit the water mainly to feed. All water mammals are good swimmers, and some can stay underwater for long periods. As water supports much of their weight, some water mammals have become huge.

Which mammals live in the sea?

Three groups of mammals live in the world's seas and oceans. They are 'cetacea' – whales, dolphins and porpoises, 'pinnipedia' – seals, sea lions and walruses, and 'sirenia' – manatees and dugongs (above right). Seals, sea lions and walruses come onto land to rest and breed, but cetaceans and sirenians spend their whole lives underwater in the sea.

Killer whale

How are beavers suited to life in the water?

Beavers are suited to their watery way of life in a number of ways. Their bodies are streamlined and their rear feet are webbed. Their eyes are protected by a special skin. Beavers also have a dense and waterproof coat that keeps them warm, both in and out of the water. But it is the tail that is the beaver's most characteristic feature. Broad, flat and scaly, the tail can be flexed up and down to drive the beaver through the water at speed, or used like a rudder to steer.

Are coypus related to beavers?

From a distance, the coypu resembles a small beaver and the two mammals are indeed relatives, both being aquatic rodents. Its stocky body is covered in thick, waterproof fur and its hind feet are webbed. The most obvious difference is that the coypu lacks the beaver's flat tail. It is, nonetheless, an excellent swimmer and spends most of its day in the water. At night, it sleeps in a bankside burrow.

Why are seals such good swimmers?

With their smooth, streamlined bodies and strong flippers, seals are superb swimmers. Thick layers of fat keep them warm and smooth out body contours. Fur seals and sea lions, or 'eared seals', swim with powerful strokes from their front flippers. 'True seals', however, such as the leopard seal (right), drive themselves through the water using their back flippers.

Dugong

Harp seal

Quick-fire Quiz

1. Which seals swim with their back flippers?
a) True seals
b) Fur seals
c) Sea lions

2. What kind of animal is a coypu?
a) A beaver
b) A rabbit
c) A rodent

3. Which water mammals are cetaceans?
a) Whales and dolphins
b) Seals and walruses
c) Manatees and dugongs

4. How does a dolphin move its tail flukes to swim?
a) Up and down
b) Side to side
c) In and out

Why does an otter have webbed feet?

An otter uses its powerful webbed feet in the same way as people use flippers – to push a lot of water aside with each swimming stroke. This helps it to swim fast, which it must do to catch its prey. Some otters also use their small, webbed front paws to catch fish underwater and most otters use them to hold food when they eat.

Why doesn't a dolphin have back legs?

To make its body more streamlined – and help it swim faster – the dolphin, over time, lost its back legs and developed a fish-like tail with two fins called 'flukes'. Unlike a fish, however, which moves its tail from side to side, a dolphin swims by beating its powerful flukes up and down. Dolphins are such strong swimmers that they can easily propel themselves out of the water.

31

Night-time Mammals

More than half the mammals in the world come out at night. They can do this because they are warm-blooded and can remain active when it is cold. Mammals may have become active at night, or 'nocturnal', to avoid daytime predators, or because it is too hot to be active by day. To find their way about in the dark and locate food, these mammals have developed excellent senses of sight, hearing and smell.

Why do bats fly at night?

Most bats come out at night to feed on the many insects that fly in the darkness. They find their prey using echo-location (below), in the same way as dolphins. With small, round bodies and large, thin wings, bats have a large surface area for their volume, so they lose heat very rapidly. To generate more heat and keep warm, they need to eat a lot of food. During one summer, a colony of one hundred bats will eat tens of millions of insects.

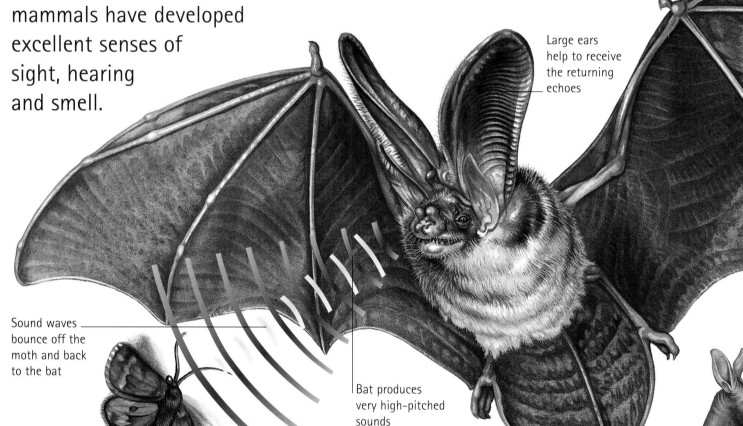

Large ears help to receive the returning echoes

Sound waves bounce off the moth and back to the bat

Bat produces very high-pitched sounds

Why do hippos leave the water at night?

As night falls, hippos leave the water and follow well-worn paths to a feeding site (left). After feeding on grasses all night, the hippos return to the water. By spending up to 18 hours a day immersed in the water, they avoid the heat of the Sun and save energy. The hippos' skin loses water very easily in the hot, dry daytime air, but the cool, moist night-time air suits them very well.

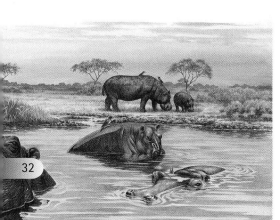

Why do badgers have a good sense of smell?

Most badgers are nocturnal and smell is their most important sense. At night, they use their sense of smell to find their way around and locate food such as earthworms. A badger may eat several hundred earthworms in just one night. An excellent sense of smell is also useful for recognizing the scent signals left by other badgers, for finding a mate and detecting danger.

Which monkey comes out at night?

The only truly nocturnal monkeys are owl monkeys, or douroucoulis. They have large eyes and can see well in low light. During the day, douroucoulis sleep in hollow trees or thick vegetation, but as night falls, they come out to catch insects and find fruit. On nights when there is a full moon, males with territories, and young males looking for a mate, will give a series of low, owl-like hooting calls.

Which night mammal likes to eat termites?

The secretive and little-known aardvark feeds on ants and termites under the cover of darkness. It uses its keen senses of smell and hearing to find food, keeping its long snout close to the ground to sniff out a meal. Aardvarks have powerful claws to rip open termite mounds and long sticky tongues to lap up the insects (left).

Which big cats hunt at night?

Lions, leopards, jaguars and tigers all hunt at night – only lions and tigers hunt during the day as well. Lions are the only big cats to hunt in groups – the others, such as the leopard (right), hunt alone. The spots and stripes on the fur of big cats help them to blend into the shadows so they can either lie in wait, or creep up on their prey without being seen.

People and Mammals

From sheep, cows and goats to pigs, camels and water buffalos, many mammals have been tamed, or 'domesticated', and bred for food or work. Those kept as pets provide human companionship and opportunities for leisure activities such as horse-riding. A few wild mammals have even adapted to living in and around our homes, taking advantage of the food, shelter and warmth of our towns and cities.

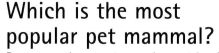

Which is the most popular pet mammal?

Dogs are the most popular pet by far. They have lived with people for more than 12,000 years and were probably the first mammals to be domesticated. The 200 or so dog breeds throughout the world are more varied in their appearance and behaviour than any other domestic animal. There are three main groups, the toy dogs, working dogs and hunting dogs. Pet dogs are all related to wild wolves and treat their owners as if they were members of their 'pack'.

Bernese mountain dog (working dog)

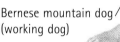

Labrador (sporting dog)

Yorkshire terrier (toy dog)

Which mammals give us wool?

Sheep (left), goats and the llama-like alpacas of South America all provide us with wool for making clothes. About 3.3 million alpacas are farmed for their fine, long wool, which grows almost down to the ground. Sheep were domesticated about 9,000 years ago by farmers who bred only those animals that did not moult their coat naturally – so that they could shear off their fleeces. Today, there are more than 200 different types of domestic sheep. Australia has about 140 million sheep in total – about seven sheep for every person in the country!

Which mammals have been trained to work for people?

Mammals such as camels, donkeys, elephants and llamas are strong animals that are used to carry heavy loads in many countries. Farmers may use oxen, water buffalo and horses to pull their ploughs. Dogs are particularly intelligent mammals and can be taught to guide blind people (left), herd sheep, sniff out drugs and explosives, and also to help the police to track down criminals. In some parts of Asia, people train otters to catch fish for them!

Which mammals compete in the Olympics?

Horses are the only mammals that take part in the Olympic Games, competing in show-jumping and cross-country events. Horses were first tamed about 6,000 years ago in Asia. People used them for their meat, milk and skins as well as to ride, carry heavy loads and pull carts and ploughs. Today, there are more than 150 breeds of horse and pony, from tiny Shetland ponies to huge shire horses. The last truly wild horses have been driven to extinction by hunting and habitat destruction.

How do apes communicate with people?

Apes cannot make the sounds to speak as we do, so scientists have taught them to communicate using signs and symbols that represent words. In the USA, scientists have taught pygmy chimpanzees, called bonobos, to understand spoken English and reply by pointing to symbols. A bonobo called Kanzi has learned several hundred symbols and can even combine them to make simple sentences.

Which mammals raid our rubbish bins at night?

Foxes and raccoons open rubbish bins with ease and feed on the food we throw away. They have adapted well to city life because they are not fussy about where they live or what they eat. They are small enough to be unobtrusive and yet large enough to travel long distances in search of food. Although too small to open bins themselves, rats also benefit from our throwaway society, and thrive in towns and cities.

Quick-fire Quiz

1. Which mammal was the first to be domesticated?
a) The horse
b) The cat
c) The dog

2. How many breeds of dog are there?
a) About 200
b) About 100
c) More than 2,000

3. How can apes communicate with people?
a) By talking
b) With signs
c) By writing

4. Which country has more sheep than people?
a) Australia
b) Wales
c) USA

Mammals in Danger

As the human population has exploded, the resulting habitat destruction and pollution have had a devastating impact on almost every species. And in the case of species with attractive coats or 'trophies' such as horns or tusks, merciless hunters have only made matters worse. As a result, about one in four mammals is endangered. Some, such as the golden lion tamarin, have been saved from the brink of extinction, but for others it may already be too late.

What is the biggest threat to the survival of mammals in the wild?

By far the biggest threat to the survival of wild mammals is the destruction of their natural habitats. Every species is perfectly adapted to a particular way of life in a particular environment. When forests are cut down, wetlands drained and grasslands ploughed up, the animals that live there are either wiped out completely or those that are left are too few in number or in too small an area to survive.

How can people help mammals?

People can help endangered mammals in many ways. Habitats at risk can be protected by becoming national parks or reserves. Using wood and paper that has come from only managed or 'sustainable' sources, and recycling as many materials as possible also reduces the human impact on our natural world. The introduction of new laws can prevent the trade in endangered species, and animal-aid groups can help with their valuable work (left). Zoos that breed threatened species in captivity and return them to the wild can also be supported in their work.

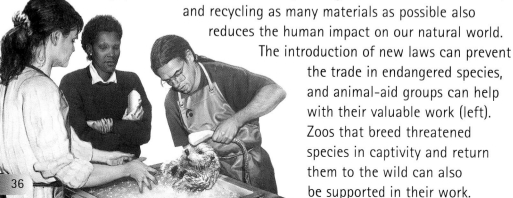

Which cats are killed for their fur?

Wild cats such as tigers, jaguars, snow leopards and ocelots are hunted for their beautiful spotted or striped skins, which are made into coats, rugs or bags. There are only about 5,000 tigers left in the wild and about the same number of snow leopards. Even where the cats are protected, poachers remain a threat.

How was the golden lion tamarin saved?

In 2001, the 1,000th golden lion tamarin was born in the Atlantic Forest of Brazil. But back in 1972, the tamarin's numbers had dwindled to just 200 in the wild and the species seemed certain to die out. The creation of the Poço das Antas reserve in 1974 began the slow process of recovery, aided by introductions from zoos and the support of local landowners. The trade in live animals for the pet trade and the killing of tamarins for sport has also been almost stopped. The next target is to increase the amount of protected forest and aim for a population of 2,000 by 2025.

Why do people kill elephants?

For decades, poachers have killed elephants for their valuable ivory tusks. During the 1980s, about 80,000 African elephants were killed each year, and by 1990, the population had crashed by 36 per cent. At this time, international trade in ivory was banned, and in Kenya, confiscated ivory worth more than £1.5 million was burned (right). But some countries believe that allowing controlled trade in ivory is the best way to protect the elephant.

When will the great apes die out?

Scientists such as Jane Goodall predict that all the 'great apes' – the gorillas, chimpanzees, orang-utans and bonobos – will be extinct in the next 20 years. One hundred years ago, there were about two million chimps living in the vast Central African rainforest – now there are at most 200,000. There are only about 15,000 bonobos left and less than 650 mountain gorillas. Wild apes are threatened by deforestation, wars and the bushmeat trade, especially in war zones, where people kill forest animals for food.

Quick-fire Quiz

1. How many mammals are threatened with extinction?
a) One in ten
b) One in four
c) One in five

2. How many mountain gorillas are left in the wild?
a) Less than 650
b) Less than 250
c) Less than 2050

3. What was the population of golden lion tamarins in 2001?
a) About 200
b) About 1,000
c) About 50

4. How many tigers are left in the wild?
a) About 15,000
b) About 10,000
c) About 5,000

Record Breakers

There are more than 4,000 species of mammal alive today. And although they all share certain characteristics, the variety in shape, size and lifestyle is breathtaking. Since the demise of the dinosaurs, mammals have spread all over Earth, under the ground, into its oceans and, in the case of bats, which make up a quarter of all mammal species, even into the skies above.

Size
- **Largest mammal:** female blue whale – more than 30 metres long and weighs more than 150 tonnes. Its tongue weighs as much as an elephant.
- **Smallest mammal:** Kitti's hog-nosed bat – 3 centimetres long and weighs 1.7–2 grammes
- **Largest land mammal:** male African elephant – 3.3 metres tall at the shoulder and weighs 5 tonnes – about the same weight as a truck. Its heart is about five times bigger than a human heart and weighs up to 21 kilogrammes – the weight of a small child.
- **Tallest mammal:** giraffe – up to 5.5 metres tall – three times the height of a tall person
- **Biggest cat:** male Siberian tiger – up to 3.3 metres long and weighs up to 306 kilogrammes. It can eat more than 35 kilogrammes of meat in one meal.
- **Longest horn:** female white rhinoceros – 1.58 metres
- **Longest tusks:** male African elephant – tusks can grow up to 3.5 metres long and may weigh up to 109 kilogrammes each. The tusks of the extinct woolly mammoth were up to 5 metres long – half as long again as the African elephant's.
- **Smallest horse:** falabella – adult less than 76 centimetres tall – only the size of many domestic dogs
- **Heaviest brain:** sperm whale – weighs up to 9 kilogrammes (six times heavier than a human brain)

Longevity
- **Human:** 100 years
- **Fin whale:** 90–100 years
- **Elephant:** 70–80 years
- **Dugong:** 73 years
- **Horse:** 35–62 years
- **Wild gorilla:** 35–45 years
- **Grizzly bear:** 35 years
- **Greater horseshoe bat:** 30 years
- **Kangaroo:** 28 years
- **Porcupine:** 27 years
- **Giraffe:** 20–25 years
- **Lion:** 15 years
- **Mongoose:** 12 years
- **Rabbit:** 6–8 years
- **European hedgehog:** 6 years
- **Dormouse:** 5 years
- **Squirrel:** 4 years
- **Mouse:** 3 years
- **Long-tailed shrew:** 12–18 months
- **Lemming:** 1 year
- **Opossum:** 1 year
- **Shrew:** 9–12 months

Movement
- **Fastest land mammal over short distances:** cheetah – can reach 90 kilometres per hour from a standing start in just three seconds
- **Fastest land mammal over long distances:** pronghorn antelope – can run at 56 kilometres per hour for about 6 kilometres
- **Slowest land mammal:** three-toed sloth – moves at 1.8–2.4 metres per minute; spends 18 hours a day asleep
- **Deepest diver:** sperm whale – dives to at least 2,000 metres and stays under for 90 minutes
- **Longest migration:** grey whale – covers a distance of 12,000–20,000 kilometres every year on migration
- **Longest bound:** kangaroo – up to 14 metres
- **Longest glide:** colugo, or flying lemur – can glide up to 136 metres between trees
- **Fastest swimmer:** killer whale – 55 kilometres per hour

Food

- **Most restricted diet**: aardwolf – eats only termites; koala – eats only eucalyptus leaves; giant panda – lives almost entirely on bamboo; vampire bat – the only mammal that feeds exclusively on blood
- **Largest appetite**: blue whale – eats up to 4 tonnes of shrimp-like krill a day; African elephant – eats 100–200 kilogrammes of plants every day and spends about 16 hours every day feeding
- **Largest prey**: killer whale – groups together to kill some of the great whales; polar bear – kills animals as large as walruses and beluga whales
- **Largest carnivore**: polar bear – weighs up to 500 kilogrammes
- **Biggest teeth**: African elephant – one tooth weighs more than a housebrick
- **Least teeth**: one-toothed shrew mouse – has only 8
- **Thirstiest mammal**: camel – can drink up to 60 litres of water in a few minutes
- **Longest tongue**: giraffe – 53 centimetres

Life cycle

- **Longest gestation period**: Asian elephant – 20–22 months
- **Shortest gestation period**: opossum and bandicoot – babies develop in only 12–13 days
- **Longest marsupial gestation period**: grey kangaroo – babies develop in 37 days
- **Largest baby**: blue whale – weighs 2–3 tonnes at birth – about half as much as an adult African elephant
- **Smallest baby**: mouse opossum – babies are only as big as grains of rice
- **Most babies**: common vole – female may have as many as 147 young in her lifetime; domestic cat – a pet called Dusty gave birth to 420 kittens
- **Largest litter**: common tenrec – up to 31 babies in one litter. The average for this species is 20 per litter
- **Smallest cub**: giant panda – cubs are only about 16 centimetres long and weigh 85–140 grammes (about the same as a small apple)
- **Shortest lactation period**: hooded seal – 4 days, but the pups double their weight in this time

Ears, eyes and noses

- **Largest ears**: African elephant – ears are almost as large as a single bedsheet and can pick up sounds from up to 8 kilometres away; fennec fox – has the largest ears of any carnivore – 15 centimetres long
- **Most sensitive nose**: dog family – a dog's sense of smell is about one million times more sensitive than our own
- **Longest nose**: African elephant – trunk is about 2.5 metres from base to tip; male northern elephant seal – 30 centimetres
- **Biggest eyes**: tarsier – has bigger eyes than any other mammal of a similar size. On a human scale, they would be the size of grapefruits
- **Worst eyesight**: Ganges river dolphin and Indus river dolphin – these species are virtually blind

Rarest mammals

- **Yangtze river dolphin**: 150
- **Asiatic lion**: less than 300
- **Siberian tiger**: 450
- **Iberian lynx**: 600
- **Mountain gorilla**: less than 650
- **Giant panda**: 1,000
- **European bison**: about 2,000
- **Black rhino**: 2,700
- **Snow leopard**: 3,500–7,000

Habitat

- **Coldest temperature**: Arctic fox – survives temperatures as low as –70°C; North American red bat – can survive when its body tissues actually turn into ice at temperatures well below freezing
- **Hottest temperatures**: fennec fox – can survive temperatures of more than 38°C in the Sahara desert
- **Most northerly**: polar bear – wanders close to the North Pole
- **Highest living**: yak – lives as high as 6,100 metres among the snowfields of the Himalayas

Index

Quick-fire Quiz ANSWERS

Page 5 A World of Mammals
1. a   2. b   3. a   4. b

Page 7 Early Mammals
1. b   2. c   3. a   4. c

Page 9 Fur Coats
1. b   2. c   3. a   4. c

Page 11 Eyes, Ears and Noses
1. c   2. a   3. b   4. c

Page 13 Run, Jump, Climb, Fly
1. b   2. c   3. a   4. c

Page 15 Food and Feeding
1. b   2. c   3. c   4. a

Page 17 Combat and Attack
1. c   2. a   3. b   4. b

Page 19 Defence
1. c   2. b   3. c   4. c

Page 21 Birth and Babies
1. b   2. c   3. c   4. c

Page 23 Living in Groups
1. b   2. a   3. c   4. b

Page 25 Keeping in Touch
1. c   2. b   3. b   4. a

Page 27 Mammal Homes
1. c   2. a   3. b   4. c

Page 29 Coping with Extremes
1. b   2. c   3. a   4. a

Page 31 Water Mammals
1. a   2. c   3. a   4. a

Page 33 Night-time Mammals
1. b   2. c   3. a   4. c

Page 35 People and Mammals
1. c   2. a   3. b   4. a

Page 37 Mammals in Danger
1. b   2. a   3. b   4. c